Meditative Coloring
Coloring Book for Adults
Jason Potash

Yap Kee Chong
8345 NW 66 ST #B7885
Miami, FL 33166

Createspace

Copyright 2015

All Rights reserved. No part of this book may be reproduced or used in any way or form or by any means whether electronic or mechanical, this means that you cannot record or photocopy any material ideas or tips that are provided in this book.

THIS BOOK BELONGS TO

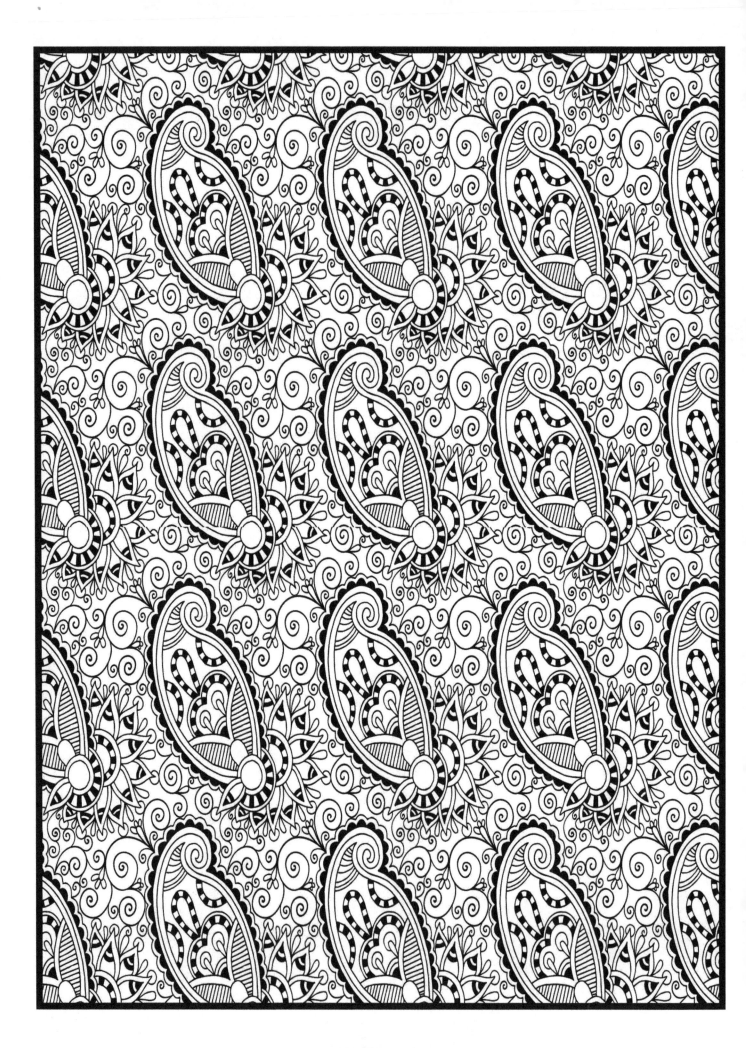

Check Out Our Other Coloring Books